The Cheerful Mindset

Cultivating a Joyful Outlook Everyday

Gerard Assey

The Cheerful Mindset:
Cultivating a Joyful Outlook Everyday

By

Gerard Assey

Published by:
Gerard Assey
19/18, Palli Arasan Street
Anna Nagar East
Chennai - 600 102

ISBN: 978-81-989262-1-0

(Image courtesy Freepik: www.Freepik.com-Thank You)

Table of Contents

Preface

Welcome to '**The Cheerful Mindset: *Cultivating a Joyful Outlook Everyday.***

This book is a comprehensive guide designed to help you cultivate a more positive and joyful outlook on life. In these pages, you will find a wealth of practical strategies, actionable steps, and inspiring examples to guide you on your journey towards developing a cheerful mind.

In today's fast-paced and often stressful world, maintaining a cheerful mindset can be challenging. However, by incorporating the principles outlined in this book into your daily life, you can learn to approach life's challenges with optimism, gratitude, and resilience.

Each chapter of this book is designed to provide you with practical tools and techniques that you can immediately apply to your own life. From understanding the importance of positivity to practicing mindful communication, each chapter offers insights and strategies to help you cultivate a more positive and cheerful mindset.

Throughout the book, you will also find personal anecdotes, case studies, and examples to illustrate the principles being discussed. These real-life examples serve to inspire and motivate you as you embark on your own journey towards a more cheerful mind.

Whether you are seeking to overcome negative thought patterns, reduce stress, or simply find more joy in your daily life, "Developing a Cheerful Mind" has something to offer you. I invite you to dive into these pages with an open mind and a willingness to explore new ways of thinking and being.

Remember, developing a cheerful mind is a journey, not a destination. It requires patience, practice, and a commitment to self-improvement. I hope that this book serves as a valuable resource on your journey towards greater happiness and well-being.
Wishing you joy, positivity, and a cheerful mind,

Understanding the Importance of Positivity

Positivity is more than just a fleeting feeling of happiness; it is a mindset that can profoundly impact our mental health and overall well-being. When we embrace positivity, we open ourselves up to a world of possibilities and experiences that can enrich our lives in countless ways.

At its core, positivity is about maintaining a hopeful and optimistic outlook on life, even in the face of challenges and adversity. It is about choosing to focus on the good in ourselves, others, and the world around us, rather than dwelling on the negative. This shift in perspective can have a powerful effect on our mental health, helping to reduce stress, anxiety, and depression.

The science behind positive thinking is fascinating and sheds light on why cultivating a positive mindset is so beneficial. Studies have shown that positive thinking can actually change the way our brains work. When we think positively, our brains release chemicals like dopamine and serotonin, which are associated with feelings of happiness and well-being. These chemicals not only make us feel good in the moment but can also have long-lasting effects on our mental and physical health.

Positivity can also improve our overall well-being and quality of life in several ways. For example, research has found that positive thinking is associated with better coping skills, resilience, and a lower risk of developing mental health disorders. Positivity can also improve our relationships, as people are naturally drawn to those who radiate positivity and optimism.

To cultivate positivity in your own life, start by paying attention to your thoughts and actively challenging negative or pessimistic thinking patterns. Replace negative thoughts with positive affirmations and gratitude for the good things in your life. Surround yourself with positive influences, such as supportive friends and uplifting media. Practice mindfulness and meditation to stay present and focused on the positive aspects of your life.

By understanding the importance of positivity and incorporating it into your daily life, you can improve your mental health, boost your overall well-being, and enjoy a more fulfilling and meaningful life.

Benefits of a Cheerful Mind to Self and Others

Maintaining a cheerful mindset offers a myriad of benefits that positively impact both ourselves and those around us. Let's explore some of these benefits in detail:

- ✓ **Improved Resilience:** A cheerful mindset enhances our ability to bounce back from adversity. For example, when faced with a setback like losing a job, a person with a cheerful mindset is more likely to view it as an opportunity for growth rather than a failure. This resilience allows them to navigate challenges with greater ease and less emotional turmoil.
- ✓ **Enhanced Emotional Health:** Positivity has a direct impact on our emotional well-being. Studies have shown that individuals who maintain a cheerful mindset are less likely to experience symptoms of anxiety and depression. For instance, someone facing a difficult situation, such as a health issue, can cope better when they focus on the positives in their life, leading to improved mental health.
- ✓ **Positive Influence on Relationships:** A cheerful mindset can significantly improve our relationships and interactions with others. For example, a person who approaches conversations with a positive attitude is more likely to be empathetic and understanding, strengthening their bonds with others. This positivity can create a supportive and

harmonious environment in both personal and professional relationships.

- ✓ **Ripple Effect of Positivity:** Positivity has a ripple effect that extends beyond individual interactions. When we maintain a cheerful mindset, we inspire others to do the same. For instance, a cheerful colleague can uplift the mood of an entire team, leading to a more positive work environment. This ripple effect can create a chain reaction of kindness and positivity that benefits the wider community.

By understanding these benefits and actively cultivating a cheerful mindset, we not only improve our own well-being but also contribute to a more positive and supportive world for everyone.

Overcoming Challenges to Positivity

Maintaining a cheerful mindset can be challenging, especially when faced with stress, negativity bias, and societal pressures. However, with the right strategies, you can overcome these obstacles and cultivate a more positive outlook on life.

Identifying Common Obstacles: Stress, negativity bias, and societal pressures are common obstacles that can hinder our ability to maintain a cheerful mindset. Stress from work, relationships, or personal challenges can overwhelm us and make it difficult to see the positive aspects of life. Negativity bias, a tendency to focus more on negative experiences than positive ones, can also impact our outlook. Additionally, societal pressures, such as comparison with others or societal standards of success, can contribute to feelings of inadequacy and negativity.

Strategies for Overcoming Challenges:

- ✓ **Mindfulness:** Mindfulness involves being present in the moment and observing your thoughts and feelings without judgment. Practicing mindfulness can help you become more aware of negative thought patterns and learn to let go of them.
- ✓ **Self-Compassion:** Self-compassion involves treating yourself with kindness and understanding, especially during difficult times. Instead of being self-critical, practice self-compassion by offering yourself the same kindness you would offer to a friend facing a similar challenge.

- ✓ **Setting Realistic Expectations:** Often, we set unrealistic expectations for ourselves, leading to feelings of failure and negativity. Set realistic goals and expectations, and celebrate small victories along the way.
- ✓ **Cultivating a Supportive Environment:** Surround yourself with positive influences and people who uplift and support you. Avoid toxic relationships and environments that contribute to negativity.

Action Plan:

- ✓ **Mindfulness Practice:** Set aside time each day for mindfulness meditation or simply take a few minutes to focus on your breath and observe your thoughts.
- ✓ **Self-Compassion Exercises:** Practice self-compassion by writing yourself a letter of encouragement or engaging in activities that bring you comfort and joy.
- ✓ **Setting Realistic Goals:** Break down larger goals into smaller, manageable tasks, and celebrate your progress along the way.
- ✓ **Creating a Supportive Network:** Reach out to friends, family, or support groups for encouragement and guidance during challenging times.

By implementing these strategies and techniques, you can overcome common obstacles to positivity and cultivate a more resilient and cheerful mindset. Remember, it's okay to seek help and support when needed, and with practice, you can navigate life's challenges with a more positive outlook.

Practical Strategies for Fostering a Positive Outlook

Developing a positive outlook is a journey that involves consciously choosing to focus on the good in life, even when faced with challenges. Here are some practical strategies to help foster a positive mindset:

Cultivating Gratitude and Appreciation: One of the most effective ways to foster positivity is by practicing gratitude. Take time each day to reflect on the things you are grateful for, no matter how small. This simple practice can shift your focus from what is lacking to what is abundant in your life.

- ✓ *Action Plan:* Keep a gratitude journal and write down three things you are grateful for each day. This can help you cultivate a habit of gratitude and train your mind to focus on the positive.

Reframing Negative Thoughts and Situations: Negative thoughts can quickly spiral out of control and lead to a pessimistic outlook. Instead of dwelling on the negative, try to reframe your thoughts in a more positive light. For example, instead of thinking, "I can't do this," reframe it as, "This is challenging, but I can learn from it."

- ✓ *Action Plan:* Practice cognitive restructuring by identifying negative thoughts and replacing them with more positive and realistic ones. This can help you develop a more optimistic outlook over time.

Engaging in Activities that Promote Joy and Happiness: Engaging in activities that bring you joy and happiness can significantly improve your overall outlook on life. This could be anything from spending time in nature, pursuing a hobby, or spending time with loved ones.

- ✓ *Action Plan:* Create a list of activities that bring you joy and make a commitment to incorporate them into your weekly routine. This can help boost your mood and enhance your overall sense of well-being.

By incorporating these practical strategies into your daily life, you can cultivate a more positive outlook and experience the benefits of a cheerful mindset. Remember, positivity is a choice, and by actively choosing to focus on the good, you can create a more fulfilling and meaningful life for yourself.

Maintaining a Cheerful Mindset in Various Situations

Maintaining a cheerful mindset can be challenging, especially when faced with different life circumstances such as work stress, relationship challenges, or personal setbacks. However, with the right strategies, you can adapt positivity to various situations and create a supportive environment that nurtures a cheerful mindset.

Adapting Positivity Strategies:

- ✓ **Work:** In a work setting, focus on the aspects of your job that you enjoy and find fulfilling. Practice gratitude for the opportunities and challenges that work brings, and seek ways to make a positive impact in your workplace.
- ✓ **Relationships:** In relationships, communication is key. Practice active listening and empathy to strengthen your connections with others. Focus on the positive aspects of your relationships and express appreciation for your loved ones.
- ✓ **Personal Challenges:** During personal challenges, such as health issues or financial difficulties, it's important to practice self-care and self-compassion. Seek support from friends, family, or a therapist, and focus on finding solutions rather than dwelling on the problem.

Tips for Staying Positive:

- ✓ **Practice Gratitude:** Keep a gratitude journal and write down three things you are grateful for each day. This can help shift your focus from what is going wrong to what is going right in your life.

- ✓ **Stay Connected:** Maintain connections with supportive friends and family members. Surrounding yourself with positive influences can help you maintain a cheerful mindset.
- ✓ **Engage in Self-Care:** Take care of your physical, mental, and emotional well-being. Engage in activities that bring you joy and relaxation, such as exercise, hobbies, or spending time in nature.

Creating a Supportive Environment:

- ✓ **Surround Yourself with Positivity:** Surround yourself with positive influences, such as uplifting music, inspiring books, or motivational quotes. These can serve as reminders to stay positive.
- ✓ **Set Boundaries:** Establish boundaries with negative influences in your life. Limit your exposure to negative news or toxic relationships, and prioritize your mental health.
- ✓ **Practice Forgiveness:** Holding onto grudges and resentment can weigh you down. Practice forgiveness, both for yourself and others, to lighten your emotional load and maintain a cheerful mindset.

Action Plan:

- ✓ **Positivity Check-In:** Regularly check in with yourself to assess your mindset. Notice any negative thought patterns and practice reframing them in a more positive light.

- ✓ **Support Network:** Build a support network of friends, family, or support groups who can uplift and encourage you during difficult times.
- ✓ **Self-Care Routine:** Create a self-care routine that includes activities that promote relaxation and joy. This could include meditation, exercise, or creative hobbies.

By implementing these strategies and tips, you can maintain a cheerful mindset in various situations and create a supportive environment that nurtures your well-being. Remember, maintaining positivity is a journey, and it's okay to seek help and support along the way.

Embracing Change

Change is inevitable in life, and learning to embrace it with a positive mindset is essential for personal growth and well-being. While change can be challenging, it also presents opportunities for new experiences and growth. Here are some practical strategies to help you embrace change and see it as an opportunity for growth:

1. **Cultivate a Growth Mindset:** Embracing change starts with adopting a growth mindset. Instead of viewing change as a threat, see it as an opportunity to learn and grow. Believe in your ability to adapt and thrive in new circumstances.

✓ *Action Plan:* Whenever you encounter a change, remind yourself that it is an opportunity for growth. Challenge yourself to see the positive aspects of the change and how it can help you learn and evolve.

2. **Practice Acceptance:** Accepting that change is a natural part of life can help you approach it with a more positive mindset. Acknowledge your feelings about the change, whether they are positive or negative, and allow yourself to process them.

✓ *Action Plan:* Take time to reflect on past changes in your life and how you adapted to them. Use these experiences to remind yourself that you have the strength and resilience to adapt to new changes.

3. **Focus on What You Can Control:** While you may not be able to control the change itself, you can control how you respond to it. Focus

on what you can control, such as your attitude, actions, and mindset.

✓ *Action Plan:* Make a list of things you can control in a changing situation. Focus on taking positive actions that align with your goals and values, rather than dwelling on things beyond your control.

4. **Seek Out Support:** Change can be easier to navigate with the support of others. Reach out to friends, family, or a support group for encouragement and advice.

✓ *Action Plan:* Share your feelings about the change with someone you trust. Seek their perspective and ask for their support in navigating the change.

5. **Stay Flexible and Open-Minded:** Approach change with a flexible and open-minded attitude. Be willing to adapt your plans and expectations as circumstances change.

✓ *Action Plan:* Practice being more flexible in your daily life. Try new things, explore new ideas, and be open to different perspectives.

6. **Focus on the Positive:** Instead of dwelling on the negative aspects of change, focus on the positive outcomes it may bring. Look for opportunities for personal growth, new experiences, and positive change.

✓ *Action Plan:* Make a list of potential positive outcomes of the change you are facing. Refer back to this list when you find yourself feeling overwhelmed by the change.

By embracing change with a positive mindset, you can navigate life's transitions more effectively and see change as an opportunity for growth and personal development. Remember that change is a natural part of life, and by staying flexible, open-minded, and focused on the positive, you can embrace change with confidence and resilience.

Cultivating Resilience

Resilience is the ability to bounce back from adversity, challenges, and setbacks. It is a crucial skill for maintaining a cheerful mindset, as it allows us to navigate life's ups and downs with grace and strength. Cultivating resilience involves developing a mindset and set of skills that enable us to overcome obstacles and grow from our experiences. Here are some strategies for building resilience:

- ✓ **Developing a Growth Mindset:** A growth mindset is the belief that our abilities and intelligence can be developed through effort and perseverance. Embracing a growth mindset can help us view challenges as opportunities for growth and learning, rather than setbacks. To develop a growth mindset, try reframing challenges as opportunities for learning and growth. For example, instead of saying "I can't do this," say "I can't do this yet, but I'm willing to learn and improve."
- ✓ **Learning from Failures:** Failure is a natural part of life, and learning to embrace it can help build resilience. Instead of viewing failure as a negative outcome, see it as a learning experience. Reflect on what went wrong, what you can learn from the experience, and how you can improve in the future. For example, if you fail to achieve a goal, instead of giving up, use it as an opportunity to reassess your approach and try again.
- ✓ **Practicing Self-Care:** Self-care is essential for maintaining resilience and overall well-being. Taking care of your physical, emotional,

and mental health can help you cope with stress and adversity. Engage in activities that help you relax and recharge, such as exercise, meditation, or spending time in nature. Prioritize self-care as a way to build resilience and maintain a cheerful mindset.

- ✓ **Building a Support Network:** Having a strong support network can help you navigate difficult times and build resilience. Surround yourself with supportive friends, family members, and mentors who can provide encouragement and guidance when you need it. Reach out to your support network when you're facing challenges and allow yourself to lean on others for support.
- ✓ **Cultivating Optimism:** Optimism is the belief that things will work out for the best, even in difficult times. Cultivating optimism can help build resilience by helping you maintain a positive outlook, even when faced with challenges. Practice reframing negative thoughts into more positive ones and focus on the things you can control rather than those you can't.
- ✓ **Setting Goals:** Setting goals can help you stay focused and motivated, even in the face of adversity. Set realistic, achievable goals that align with your values and aspirations. Break your goals down into smaller, manageable steps and celebrate your progress along the way. This can help build resilience and keep you motivated to continue moving forward.

Building resilience takes time and effort, but it is a skill that can be developed with practice. By developing a growth mindset, learning from failures, practicing self-care, building a support network, cultivating optimism, and setting goals, you can build resilience and maintain a cheerful mindset even in the face of life's challenges.

Managing Stress

Stress is a common part of life, but when left unchecked, it can take a toll on our mental and physical health. Learning how to manage stress effectively is essential for maintaining a cheerful mindset and overall well-being. Here are some practical tips and techniques for managing stress:

- ✓ **Meditation:** Meditation is a powerful tool for managing stress and promoting relaxation. It involves focusing your mind on a particular object, thought, or activity to train attention and awareness, and achieve a mentally clear and emotionally calm and stable state. Start by finding a quiet place to sit or lie down, close your eyes, and focus on your breath. Try to let go of any thoughts or distractions and simply be present in the moment. Even just a few minutes of meditation each day can help reduce stress and promote a sense of calm.
- ✓ **Deep Breathing Exercises:** Deep breathing exercises can help calm the mind and body by activating the body's relaxation response. To practice deep breathing, sit or lie down in a comfortable position and place one hand on your abdomen and the other on your chest. Inhale slowly and deeply through your nose, allowing your abdomen to rise as you fill your lungs with air. Exhale slowly through your mouth, allowing your abdomen to fall. Repeat this process several times, focusing on your breath and letting go of any tension or stress.
- ✓ **Progressive Muscle Relaxation:** Progressive muscle relaxation is a technique that involves

tensing and then relaxing different muscle groups in the body to reduce stress and promote relaxation. Start by sitting or lying down in a comfortable position. Begin at your feet and work your way up, tensing each muscle group for a few seconds and then releasing. Pay attention to how each muscle group feels when tense and when relaxed. This can help you become more aware of tension in your body and learn to release it.

- ✓ **Mindfulness:** Mindfulness is the practice of being fully present and engaged in the moment, without judgment. Mindfulness can help reduce stress by allowing you to observe your thoughts and feelings without getting caught up in them. To practice mindfulness, choose an activity that you can do mindfully, such as eating, walking, or washing dishes. Focus on the sensations of the activity, such as the taste of your food or the feeling of your feet on the ground. Whenever you notice your mind wandering, gently bring it back to the present moment.
- ✓ **Time Management Strategies:** Poor time management can be a significant source of stress. To manage your time more effectively, try prioritizing your tasks, breaking them down into smaller, more manageable steps, and setting realistic deadlines. Use tools such as to-do lists, calendars, and planners to help you stay organized and on track. Learn to say no to tasks or commitments that are not essential or that will overwhelm you.
- ✓ **Physical Activity:** Regular physical activity can help reduce stress and improve your

mood. Exercise releases endorphins, which are chemicals in the brain that act as natural painkillers and mood elevators. Find an activity that you enjoy, such as walking, running, or dancing, and make it a regular part of your routine.

- ✓ **Healthy Lifestyle Choices:** Eating a healthy diet, getting enough sleep, and avoiding excessive alcohol and caffeine can help reduce stress and improve your overall well-being. Try to eat a balanced diet rich in fruits, vegetables, whole grains, and lean proteins, and aim for 7-9 hours of quality sleep each night.
- ✓ **Seeking Support:** If you're feeling overwhelmed by stress, don't hesitate to seek support from a mental health professional. They can help you develop coping strategies and provide you with the support you need to manage your stress effectively.

By incorporating these practical tips and techniques into your daily routine, you can effectively manage stress and maintain a cheerful mindset, even in the face of life's challenges. Remember, managing stress is a skill that takes practice, so be patient with yourself and experiment with different techniques to find what works best for you.

Nurturing Relationships

Healthy relationships are essential for maintaining a cheerful mindset and overall well-being. Whether with friends, family, or partners, nurturing relationships can provide support, love, and a sense of belonging. Here are some practical tips for building and maintaining strong connections:

1. **Communicate Openly and Honestly:** Effective communication is key to nurturing relationships. Be open and honest with your thoughts and feelings, and encourage others to do the same. Listen actively to what others have to say and show empathy and understanding.

✓ *Action Plan:* Schedule regular check-ins with your loved ones to discuss your feelings, concerns, and joys. Practice active listening by focusing on what the other person is saying without interrupting or judging.

2. **Show Appreciation and Gratitude:** Expressing appreciation and gratitude for the people in your life can strengthen your relationships and boost your own happiness. Take time to thank your loved ones for their support and kindness.

✓ *Action Plan:* Write a heartfelt letter or note to someone you care about, expressing your gratitude for their presence in your life. Make an effort to verbally acknowledge the things you appreciate about them regularly.

3. **Spend Quality Time Together:** Quality time spent with loved ones helps strengthen bonds and create lasting memories. Make an effort to

prioritize time with friends, family, and partners, even amid busy schedules.

- ✓ *Action Plan:* Plan regular activities or outings with your loved ones that you both enjoy. This could be a weekly dinner, a movie night, or a weekend getaway.

4. **Practice Forgiveness:** Holding onto grudges can strain relationships and negatively impact your mental health. Practice forgiveness and let go of past grievances to nurture healthy, positive relationships.

- ✓ *Action Plan:* Reflect on any past conflicts or disagreements you've had with loved ones and consider reaching out to them to discuss and resolve any lingering issues.

5. **Support Each Other's Goals:** Encourage and support your loved ones in pursuing their goals and dreams. Celebrate their successes and offer a helping hand when they face challenges.

- ✓ *Action Plan:* Have a conversation with your loved ones about their goals and aspirations. Discuss how you can support each other in achieving them and set realistic expectations for how you can help.

6. **Set Boundaries:** Setting healthy boundaries is essential for maintaining healthy relationships. Be clear about your needs and limits, and respect those of others.

- ✓ *Action Plan:* Have a conversation with your loved ones about your boundaries and ask them to do the same. Respect each other's boundaries and communicate openly if they are ever crossed.

7. **Seek Professional Help When Needed:** If you're struggling in your relationships, don't hesitate to seek support from a therapist or counselor. They can help you navigate relationship challenges and develop healthier communication patterns.

✓ *Action Plan:* If you feel that your relationships could benefit from professional guidance, research therapists or counselors in your area and schedule an appointment to discuss your concerns.

By implementing these tips and strategies, you can nurture healthy, positive relationships that contribute to a cheerful mindset and overall well-being. Remember that relationships require effort and commitment from both parties, so be patient and compassionate as you navigate your connections with others.

Setting Boundaries

Setting boundaries is crucial for maintaining your mental health and well-being, as it helps you establish clear guidelines for how you want to be treated by others. Boundaries can be physical, emotional, or mental, and they are essential for fostering healthy relationships. Here are some practical tips for setting and maintaining boundaries:

1. **Identify Your Limits:** Take some time to reflect on your needs, values, and limits. What behaviors or actions are acceptable to you, and which ones are not? Knowing your limits is the first step in setting boundaries.

✓ *Action Plan:* Make a list of your personal boundaries in different areas of your life, such as work, relationships, and personal space. This will help you clarify your boundaries and communicate them effectively.

2. **Communicate Your Boundaries Clearly:** Once you've identified your boundaries, communicate them clearly and assertively to others. Use "I" statements to express your needs and feelings without blaming or criticizing.

✓ *Action Plan:* Practice assertive communication by role-playing with a friend or writing down how you would assertively communicate your boundaries in different situations.

3. **Be Consistent:** Consistency is key to maintaining boundaries. Once you've set a boundary, stick to it, even if it's difficult or uncomfortable. Consistency helps establish trust and respect in your relationships.

- ✓ *Action Plan:* Practice saying "no" to requests or behaviors that violate your boundaries. Start with small, low-stakes situations to build your confidence in asserting your boundaries.

4. **Set Consequences:** Clearly communicate the consequences of crossing your boundaries. Consequences should be reasonable and proportionate to the violation of your boundaries.

- ✓ *Action Plan:* Think about the consequences you're willing to enforce if someone crosses your boundaries. For example, if a friend consistently shows up late for plans, you might decide to limit future invitations.

5. **Practice Self-Care:** Setting boundaries also means taking care of yourself and prioritizing your well-being. Practice self-care activities that help you recharge and maintain your boundaries.

- ✓ *Action Plan:* Make a list of self-care activities that help you relax and rejuvenate. Schedule regular self-care time into your routine to ensure you're meeting your own needs.

6. **Seek Support:** If you're struggling to set or maintain boundaries, seek support from a therapist, counselor, or trusted friend. They can offer guidance and encouragement as you work on establishing healthy boundaries.

- ✓ *Action Plan:* Reach out to someone you trust and share your struggles with setting boundaries. Ask for their support and guidance in enforcing your boundaries.

Setting boundaries is an ongoing process that requires self-awareness, assertiveness, and self-care. By practicing these strategies, you can establish healthy boundaries that protect your mental health and well-being, and foster positive and respectful relationships.

Practicing Self-Compassion

Self-compassion is the practice of treating yourself with kindness, understanding, and acceptance, especially in times of difficulty or failure. It is an essential component of maintaining a cheerful mindset, as it allows you to be more forgiving and understanding of yourself. Here are some practical strategies for practicing self-compassion:

- ✓ **Treat Yourself with Kindness:** Be mindful of the way you talk to yourself and treat yourself with the same kindness and compassion that you would offer to a friend. Avoid self-criticism and negative self-talk.
- ✓ *Action Plan:* Whenever you catch yourself being self-critical, pause and reframe your thoughts. Instead of criticizing yourself, offer yourself words of kindness and encouragement.

1. **Acknowledge Your Emotions:** Allow yourself to acknowledge and validate your emotions, even if they are difficult or uncomfortable. Recognize that it is normal to experience a range of emotions and that it is okay to feel what you are feeling.

- ✓ *Action Plan:* Practice mindfulness by taking a few moments each day to check in with yourself and identify how you are feeling. Allow yourself to sit with your emotions without judgment.

2. **Practice Self-Forgiveness:** Forgiving yourself for past mistakes and failures is an important part of practicing self-compassion.

Recognize that everyone makes mistakes and that they do not define your worth.

- ✓ *Action Plan:* Think of a mistake or failure that you are holding onto. Write yourself a letter of forgiveness, acknowledging the mistake, accepting it, and forgiving yourself.

3. **Cultivate Self-Kindness:** Engage in activities that promote self-care and self-kindness. This could include taking a bubble bath, going for a walk in nature, or spending time doing something you love.

- ✓ *Action Plan:* Create a list of activities that make you feel good and that you can turn to when you need a boost of self-kindness. Refer to this list whenever you need a pick-me-up.

4. **Practice Mindfulness:** Mindfulness can help you become more aware of your thoughts and feelings and can help you respond to them with compassion rather than judgment.

- ✓ *Action Plan:* Practice mindfulness meditation for a few minutes each day. Focus on your breath and observe any thoughts or feelings that arise without judgment.

5. **Seek Support:** If you are struggling to practice self-compassion, seek support from a therapist, counselor, or trusted friend or family member. They can offer guidance and support as you work on developing self-compassion.

- ✓ *Action Plan:* Reach out to someone you trust and share your struggles with practicing self-compassion. Ask for their support and guidance as you work on cultivating more compassion for yourself.

By practicing self-compassion, you can cultivate a more positive and cheerful mindset, even in the face of challenges and difficulties. Remember that self-compassion is a skill that takes time and practice to develop, so be patient with yourself as you work on incorporating these strategies into your life.

Finding Meaning and Purpose

Finding meaning and purpose in life is essential for overall well-being and a cheerful mindset. When you have a sense of purpose, you feel more fulfilled, motivated, and resilient in the face of challenges. Here are some practical strategies to help you discover your passions and align your actions with your values:

1. **Reflect on Your Values:** Start by reflecting on what matters most to you in life. Consider the principles, beliefs, and ideals that guide your decisions and actions. Your values can provide clues to your passions and purpose.

✓ *Action Plan:* Take some time to write down your core values. Consider how these values influence your daily life and decisions. Use them as a guide to align your actions with your values.

2. **Explore Your Interests:** Pay attention to the activities that bring you joy, excitement, and fulfillment. These interests can be a clue to your passions and can help you uncover your purpose.

✓ *Action Plan:* Make a list of activities that you enjoy doing in your free time. Look for patterns or themes among these activities. Consider how you can incorporate more of these activities into your daily life.

3. **Set Meaningful Goals:** Setting goals that align with your values and interests can give you a sense of purpose and direction. Choose goals that challenge you and inspire you to grow.

- ✓ *Action Plan:* Identify one meaningful goal that you would like to achieve in the next month, year, or five years. Break this goal down into smaller, actionable steps and create a plan to achieve it.

4. **Volunteer or Help Others:** Helping others can provide a sense of purpose and fulfillment. Volunteer for causes that are meaningful to you or offer to help friends, family, or community members in need.

- ✓ *Action Plan:* Research local volunteer opportunities or organizations that align with your values and interests. Dedicate a few hours each month to volunteering and see how it impacts your sense of purpose.

5. **Find Meaning in Your Work:** If possible, try to find meaning and purpose in your work. This could involve aligning your career with your values, pursuing a passion project, or finding ways to make a positive impact in your workplace.

- ✓ *Action Plan:* Reflect on how your work aligns with your values and interests. Consider ways you can make your work more meaningful, such as taking on new challenges, seeking out mentorship opportunities, or pursuing further education or training.

6. **Practice Mindfulness:** Mindfulness can help you stay present and engaged in your life, which can lead to a greater sense of purpose and meaning. Practice mindfulness through meditation, yoga, or simply by being more aware of your thoughts and feelings.

- ✓ *Action Plan:* Dedicate a few minutes each day to practice mindfulness. Sit quietly and focus on your breath, or engage in a mindful activity such as walking or eating. Notice any thoughts or feelings that arise without judgment.

Finding meaning and purpose in life is an ongoing process that requires self-reflection, exploration, and action. By following these strategies and staying open to new experiences, you can discover your passions, align your actions with your values, and cultivate a more meaningful and purposeful life.

Cultivating Optimism

Optimism is the belief that things will work out for the best, even in difficult times. Cultivating optimism is essential for maintaining a cheerful mindset and a positive outlook on life. Here are some practical tips for cultivating optimism:

1. **Reframe Negative Thoughts:** When faced with negative thoughts or situations, try to reframe them in a more positive light. Instead of focusing on what could go wrong, focus on what could go right.

✓ *Action Plan:* Identify a negative thought you've had recently and challenge it by finding a more positive and realistic perspective. For example, if you're worried about a presentation at work, reframe your thought from "I'll probably mess up" to "I've prepared well and can handle this."

2. **Focus on Solutions:** Instead of dwelling on problems, focus on finding solutions. Approach challenges with a problem-solving mindset and believe in your ability to overcome obstacles.

✓ *Action Plan:* The next time you encounter a problem, brainstorm possible solutions and take proactive steps to address it. Focus on the actions you can take rather than feeling overwhelmed by the problem itself.

3. **Practice Gratitude:** Cultivating a sense of gratitude can help shift your focus from what's lacking to what you have. Regularly practice gratitude by reflecting on the things you're thankful for in your life.

- ✓ *Action Plan:* Keep a gratitude journal and write down three things you're grateful for each day. This practice can help train your brain to focus on the positive aspects of your life.

4. **Surround Yourself with Positivity:** Surround yourself with positive people and influences that uplift and inspire you. Limit exposure to negative news or media that can dampen your optimism.

- ✓ *Action Plan:* Identify positive influences in your life, such as friends, family, or mentors, and make an effort to spend more time with them. Consider unfollowing social media accounts that promote negativity.

5. **Maintain a Sense of Humor:** Humor can be a powerful tool for cultivating optimism and reducing stress. Find ways to laugh and see the lighter side of life's challenges.

- ✓ *Action Plan:* Watch a funny movie or TV show, read a humorous book, or spend time with friends who make you laugh. Laughter can help shift your perspective and boost your mood.

6. **Practice Positive Self-Talk:** Pay attention to the way you talk to yourself and challenge negative self-talk. Replace negative thoughts with positive affirmations and beliefs.

- ✓ *Action Plan:* Identify a negative belief you have about yourself and replace it with a positive affirmation. For example, replace "I'm not good enough" with "I am capable and deserving of success."

Cultivating optimism is a mindset that can be developed with practice and persistence. By incorporating these strategies into your daily life, you can cultivate a more optimistic outlook and maintain a cheerful mindset, even in challenging times.

Practicing Mindful Communication

Effective communication is the cornerstone of healthy relationships, as it allows individuals to express their thoughts, feelings, and needs clearly and respectfully. Mindful communication involves being fully present and attentive during conversations, speaking honestly and respectfully, and expressing empathy towards others. Here are some practical strategies for practicing mindful communication:

1. **Practice Active Listening:** Active listening involves fully concentrating on what the other person is saying, rather than thinking about your response. Show that you're listening by making eye contact, nodding, and paraphrasing what the other person has said.

✓ *Action Plan:* Practice active listening in your daily conversations. Set aside distractions, such as your phone or computer, and focus fully on the speaker. Repeat back what you've heard to ensure understanding.

2. **Speak Honestly and Respectfully:** When communicating your thoughts and feelings, be honest and direct, but also respectful. Use "I" statements to express your feelings without blaming or accusing the other person.

✓ *Action Plan:* Practice expressing your thoughts and feelings using "I" statements. For example, instead of saying "You never listen to me," try saying "I feel unheard when I don't get a chance to share my thoughts."

3. **Express Empathy:** Empathy is the ability to understand and share the feelings of another

person. When communicating, try to put yourself in the other person's shoes and acknowledge their feelings.

- ✓ *Action Plan:* Practice expressing empathy by reflecting on how others might be feeling in different situations. When someone shares their feelings with you, validate their emotions and show that you understand.

4. **Be Mindful of Nonverbal Communication:** Nonverbal cues, such as body language and facial expressions, can convey a lot of information during a conversation. Be mindful of your own nonverbal cues and pay attention to those of the other person.

- ✓ *Action Plan:* Practice observing nonverbal cues in your conversations. Notice how your body language and facial expressions impact the conversation, and try to align them with your verbal messages.

5. **Practice Patience:** Communication is a two-way street, and it's important to be patient and respectful, even when emotions are running high. Take a deep breath and pause before responding to ensure your words are thoughtful and considerate.

- ✓ *Action Plan:* When you feel yourself becoming impatient during a conversation, take a moment to pause and breathe deeply. This can help you respond more calmly and effectively.

6. **Seek Feedback:** Regularly seek feedback from others on your communication style. Ask for specific examples of times when your communication was effective or could be improved.

- ✓ *Action Plan:* Reach out to a trusted friend, family member, or colleague and ask for feedback on your communication style. Use their input to identify areas for improvement and practice implementing changes.

Practicing mindful communication takes effort and practice, but it can greatly improve the quality of your relationships and interactions with others. By incorporating these strategies into your daily communication, you can become a more effective and empathetic communicator.

Celebrating Progress

Celebrating your progress, no matter how small, is crucial for maintaining a cheerful mindset and staying motivated on your journey toward your goals. It's important to acknowledge your achievements and give yourself credit for the hard work and effort you've put in. Here are some practical strategies for celebrating your progress:

1. **Acknowledge Your Achievements:** Take time to reflect on your accomplishments, no matter how small they may seem. Acknowledge the effort and dedication you've put into reaching your goals.

✓ *Action Plan:* Keep a journal of your achievements, big and small. Write down what you accomplished, how it made you feel, and what you learned from the experience.

2. **Reward Yourself:** Treat yourself to a reward when you reach a milestone or achieve a goal. This could be something simple, like a favorite meal or a relaxing activity, or something more substantial, like a weekend getaway or a new purchase.

✓ *Action Plan:* Create a list of rewards that you can give yourself for reaching different milestones. Refer to this list when you achieve a goal and choose a reward that feels meaningful to you.

3. **Share Your Successes:** Share your achievements with others and allow yourself to be proud of your accomplishments. Celebrate with friends, family, or colleagues who support you and cheer you on.

- ✓ *Action Plan:* Share your achievements on social media or in a group chat with friends and family. Allow yourself to bask in the congratulations and positive feedback you receive.

4. **Create a Ritual:** Develop a ritual or tradition to celebrate your achievements. This could be something as simple as lighting a candle or writing a letter to yourself congratulating yourself on your success.

- ✓ *Action Plan:* Create a ritual that feels meaningful to you and that you can use to celebrate your achievements. Repeat this ritual each time you reach a milestone to create a sense of accomplishment and celebration.

5. **Set New Goals:** Celebrate your achievements by setting new goals and challenges for yourself. This keeps you motivated and gives you something to strive for.

- ✓ *Action Plan:* After celebrating an achievement, take some time to set new goals for yourself. Choose goals that are challenging but achievable, and that align with your values and interests.

6. **Practice Gratitude:** Take a moment to express gratitude for the progress you've made and the opportunities that have come your way. Gratitude can help you stay positive and motivated.

- ✓ *Action Plan:* At the end of each day, write down three things you're grateful for related to your progress and achievements. This can help you stay focused on the positive aspects of your journey.

By celebrating your progress and achievements, you can maintain a cheerful mindset and stay motivated on your journey toward your goals. Remember to acknowledge your hard work and dedication, and to celebrate even the smallest successes along the way.

Personal Anecdotes and Case Studies

Real-life stories of individuals who have successfully developed a cheerful mindset can provide valuable insights and inspiration for readers. These stories illustrate that developing a positive outlook is achievable, even in the face of adversity. Here are a few examples:

- ✓ **Sarah's Story:** Sarah was facing a challenging time in her life. She had lost her job and was struggling to make ends meet. Instead of succumbing to despair, Sarah decided to focus on the things she was grateful for. She started a gratitude journal and made a conscious effort to find joy in small things. Over time, Sarah's mindset shifted, and she was able to find a new job and regain her financial stability. Sarah's story teaches us the power of gratitude and how it can transform our outlook on life.
- ✓ **David's Journey:** David had always been a pessimistic person, constantly focusing on the negative aspects of life. However, after attending a mindfulness retreat, David learned to be more present and aware of his thoughts. He practiced mindfulness regularly and gradually noticed a shift in his mindset. David became more optimistic and began to see opportunities where he once saw obstacles. David's journey demonstrates the transformative power of mindfulness in cultivating a positive outlook.

- ✓ **Maria's Experience:** Maria was diagnosed with a chronic illness that significantly impacted her daily life. Instead of letting the illness define her, Maria chose to focus on what she could control. She adopted a healthy lifestyle, engaged in activities that brought her joy, and sought support from friends and family. Despite her illness, Maria maintained a cheerful and positive attitude, inspiring those around her. Maria's experience teaches us the importance of resilience and the ability to find joy in difficult circumstances.

These anecdotes highlight the resilience and strength of individuals who have successfully developed a cheerful mindset. They demonstrate that positivity is not just a personality trait but a skill that can be learned and cultivated. Readers can draw inspiration from these stories and apply the lessons learned to their own lives. By practicing gratitude, mindfulness, and resilience, readers can develop a more positive outlook and navigate life's challenges with a cheerful mindset.

31 Positive Affirmations- One for Each Day of the Month

Here's a list of 31 positive affirmations that you can use, one for each day of the month:

1. *Today, I choose happiness and abundance in all areas of my life.*
2. *I am capable of achieving great things, and I believe in my abilities.*
3. *I radiate love and positivity, and it comes back to me in abundance.*
4. *I am grateful for all the blessings in my life, both big and small.*
5. *I trust that everything is unfolding for my highest good.*
6. *I am deserving of love, happiness, and success.*
7. *I choose to let go of negativity and embrace positivity in every situation.*
8. *I am surrounded by supportive and loving people who uplift me.*
9. *I am confident in my decisions and trust my intuition to guide me.*
10. *I am resilient and can overcome any challenge that comes my way.*
11. *I am a magnet for success and prosperity.*
12. *I am healthy, strong, and full of energy.*
13. *I am at peace with who I am and where I am in life.*
14. *I forgive myself for past mistakes and learn from them.*
15. *I am worthy of all the good things that come into my life.*
16. *I choose to see the good in myself and others.*

17. I am open to new opportunities and adventures.
18. I trust the universe to provide me with everything I need.
19. I release all fears and doubts and embrace faith and positivity.
20. I am a source of light and positivity in the world.
21. I am constantly growing and evolving into the best version of myself.
22. I am surrounded by abundance, and I am grateful for all that I have.
23. I trust in the process of life and know that everything happens for a reason.
24. I am enough just as I am, and I deserve love and respect.
25. I radiate confidence, self-love, and inner peace.
26. I am the architect of my life, and I choose to build it with love and positivity.
27. I attract positive and uplifting experiences into my life.
28. I am free to create the life of my dreams, and I do so with joy and gratitude.
29. I am a beacon of positivity, and my light shines brightly for all to see.
30. I am grateful for the gift of today and look forward to the blessings of tomorrow.
31. I am exactly where I need to be, and I trust in the divine plan for my life.

30 Things to do to Maintain a Cheerful Mind

Here's a list of 30 things you could do to maintain a cheerful mind- explained in detail with examples

1. **Practice Gratitude:** Take a few minutes each day to write down three things you are grateful for. This simple practice can shift your focus from what is lacking to what is abundant in your life. For example, you could be grateful for a sunny day, a delicious meal, or a supportive friend.
2. **Engage in Physical Activity:** Regular exercise releases endorphins, which are known as "feel-good" hormones. Whether it's going for a walk, doing yoga, or dancing, physical activity can boost your mood and improve your overall well-being.
3. **Connect with Nature:** Spending time outdoors can have a calming effect on the mind and body. Take a walk in a park, go for a hike, or simply sit outside and soak up the sun and fresh air.
4. **Practice Mindfulness:** Mindfulness involves being present in the moment and observing your thoughts and feelings without judgment. Mindfulness can help reduce stress and anxiety and promote a sense of calm and clarity.
5. **Limit Social Media Use:** While social media can be a great way to stay connected, it can also be a source of negativity and comparison.

Limit your social media use and focus on activities that bring you joy and fulfillment.

6. **Practice Self-Compassion:** Treat yourself with kindness and understanding, especially during difficult times. Instead of being self-critical, practice self-compassion by offering yourself the same kindness you would offer to a friend facing a similar challenge.
7. **Laugh Often:** Laughter is a powerful antidote to stress and can help improve your mood. Watch a funny movie, listen to a comedy podcast, or spend time with friends who make you laugh.
8. **Practice Deep Breathing:** Deep breathing can help calm the mind and body. Take a few minutes to focus on your breath, inhaling deeply through your nose and exhaling slowly through your mouth.
9. **Engage in Creative Activities:** Engaging in creative activities such as painting, writing, or crafting can help you express your emotions and boost your mood. You don't have to be an artist to enjoy the benefits of creativity.
10. **Spend Time with Loved Ones:** Spending time with friends and family who uplift and support you can have a positive impact on your mood. Whether it's a phone call, a video chat, or an in-person visit, connecting with loved ones can brighten your day.
11. **Practice Random Acts of Kindness:** Doing something kind for someone else can boost your mood and create a ripple effect of positivity. It could be as simple as holding the door open for someone or buying a coffee for the person behind you in line.

12. **Listen to Music:** Music has the power to uplift your mood and evoke positive emotions. Create a playlist of your favorite songs and listen to it whenever you need a mood boost.
13. **Practice Forgiveness:** Holding onto grudges and resentment can weigh you down. Practice forgiveness, both for yourself and others, to lighten your emotional load and maintain a cheerful mindset.
14. **Set Realistic Goals:** Setting and achieving goals can boost your confidence and sense of accomplishment. Start small and gradually increase the complexity of your goals as you build momentum.
15. **Get Enough Sleep:** Lack of sleep can negatively impact your mood and mental health. Aim for 7-9 hours of quality sleep each night to ensure you wake up feeling refreshed and energized.
16. **Eat a Balanced Diet:** A healthy diet rich in fruits, vegetables, whole grains, and lean proteins can help support your mood and overall well-being. Avoiding excessive sugar and processed foods can also help stabilize your mood.
17. **Practice Positive Self-Talk:** Replace negative self-talk with positive affirmations. Instead of saying, "I can't do this," say, "I am capable and competent." Positive self-talk can help boost your confidence and improve your outlook.
18. **Volunteer:** Giving back to others can bring a sense of fulfillment and purpose. Look for volunteer opportunities in your community or

online that align with your interests and values.

19. **Learn Something New:** Stimulate your mind by learning something new. Whether it's a new language, a musical instrument, or a hobby, challenging yourself intellectually can help keep your mind sharp and engaged.
20. **Practice Gratitude:** Keep a gratitude journal and write down three things you are grateful for each day. This can help you cultivate a habit of gratitude and train your mind to focus on the positive.
21. **Practice Positive Visualization:** Visualize yourself achieving your goals and living your best life. This can help you stay motivated and focused on the positive outcomes you want to achieve.
22. **Surround Yourself with Positivity:** Surround yourself with positive influences, such as uplifting music, inspiring books, or motivational quotes. These can serve as reminders to stay positive.
23. **Set Boundaries:** Establish boundaries with negative influences in your life. Limit your exposure to negative news or toxic relationships, and prioritize your mental health.
24. **Practice Forgiveness:** Holding onto grudges and resentment can weigh you down. Practice forgiveness, both for yourself and others, to lighten your emotional load and maintain a cheerful mindset.
25. **Spend Time in Nature:** Nature has a calming effect on the mind and body. Spend time outdoors, whether it's going for a walk in the

park or simply sitting in your backyard, to boost your mood and reduce stress.

26. **Practice Mindfulness:** Mindfulness involves being present in the moment and observing your thoughts and feelings without judgment. Practicing mindfulness can help you stay grounded and focused on the present moment.
27. **Engage in Physical Activity:** Regular exercise releases endorphins, which are chemicals in the brain that act as natural painkillers and mood elevators. Exercise can help reduce feelings of stress and anxiety and improve your overall well-being.
28. **Connect with Others:** Maintaining social connections is important for mental health and well-being. Reach out to friends and family members, even if it's just for a quick chat or video call.
29. **Practice Self-Care:** Taking care of yourself is essential for maintaining a cheerful mindset. Set aside time each day to do something you enjoy, whether it's reading a book, taking a bath, or going for a walk.
30. **Seek Professional Help:** If you're struggling to maintain a cheerful mindset, don't hesitate to seek help from a mental health professional. They can provide you with the support and guidance you need to improve your mental health and well-being.

12 Daily Habits of Cheerful/ Joyful People

1. **Practice Gratitude:** Joyful people often start or end their day by acknowledging the things they are grateful for. This habit shifts focus from what's lacking to what's present, fostering contentment and positivity.

✓ *Example:* Keeping a gratitude journal and writing down three things you're grateful for each day, no matter how small, can help cultivate a more joyful outlook.

2. **Mindful Living:** Being present in the moment and fully engaging with whatever you're doing can enhance joy and reduce stress. Mindfulness helps joyful people appreciate life's simple pleasures.

✓ *Example:* Paying full attention while eating a meal, noticing the flavors, textures, and aromas, can turn a routine activity into a joyful experience.

3. **Regular Exercise:** Physical activity releases endorphins, the body's natural feel-good chemicals, promoting a sense of well-being and joy.

✓ *Example:* Going for a daily walk, jog, or practicing yoga can uplift mood and increase overall happiness.

4. **Cultivating Positive Relationships:** Joyful people surround themselves with supportive, uplifting individuals who contribute positively to their lives.

- ✓ *Example:* Spending quality time with loved ones, sharing laughter and creating cherished memories, can boost happiness levels.

5. **Acts of Kindness:** Helping others and being of service can generate feelings of joy and fulfillment.
   - ✓ *Example:* Volunteering at a local charity or simply offering a kind word to a stranger can create a sense of happiness.
6. **Limiting Screen Time:** Excessive screen time can contribute to feelings of isolation and reduce happiness. Joyful people balance screen time with real-world interactions.
   - ✓ *Example:* Setting aside specific times to check emails and social media, allowing for more meaningful, present interactions with others.
7. **Embracing Nature:** Spending time outdoors and connecting with nature can rejuvenate the spirit and enhance feelings of joy.
   - ✓ *Example:* Going for a hike, visiting a park, or simply sitting in a garden can provide a sense of peace and joy.
8. **Mindful Breathing:** Taking time to focus on deep, mindful breathing can calm the mind and body, promoting feelings of joy and relaxation.
   - ✓ *Example:* Practicing deep breathing exercises, such as diaphragmatic breathing, can reduce stress and increase feelings of joy.
9. **Creative Expression:** Engaging in creative activities, such as painting, writing, or playing music, can be a source of joy and fulfillment.
   - ✓ *Example:* Setting aside time each day for a creative hobby can bring a sense of accomplishment and joy.

10. **Maintaining a Healthy Lifestyle:** Eating a balanced diet, getting enough sleep, and prioritizing self-care contribute to overall well-being and joy.

✓ *Example:* Ensuring you get enough rest, eating nourishing foods, and engaging in activities that promote relaxation, such as meditation or reading, can support a joyful mindset.

11. **Practicing Forgiveness:** Joyful people are often quick to forgive others and themselves. Holding onto grudges or past mistakes can weigh heavily on the mind and prevent feelings of joy.

✓ *Example:* Making a conscious effort to let go of resentments and practice forgiveness can lead to greater peace and joy.

12. **Setting Daily Intentions:** Starting the day with a clear intention or purpose can set a positive tone and guide actions throughout the day, fostering a sense of fulfillment and joy.

✓ *Example:* Setting an intention to approach each interaction with kindness and compassion can create a more positive and joyful experience for yourself and others.

Exercises and Action Plans

To help readers implement the strategies discussed in this book and develop a cheerful mindset, we have created practical exercises and action plans. These exercises are designed to be accessible to anyone and can be easily incorporated into daily life. By following these action plans and tracking your progress, you can cultivate a more positive outlook and experience the benefits of a cheerful mindset.

Gratitude Journal: Start a gratitude journal and write down three things you are grateful for each day. This simple exercise can help shift your focus from what is lacking to what is abundant in your life. Try to be specific and reflect on why you are grateful for each thing.

- ✓ *Action Plan:* Set aside a few minutes each day to write in your gratitude journal. Choose a consistent time, such as before bed or first thing in the morning, to make it a habit.

Positive Affirmations: Create a list of positive affirmations that resonate with you. Repeat these affirmations daily to reinforce positive thinking and cultivate a more optimistic outlook.

- ✓ *Action Plan:* Choose a few affirmations to focus on each day. Repeat them aloud or write them down to internalize the positive messages.

Mindfulness Meditation: Practice mindfulness meditation to become more present and aware of your thoughts and feelings. Focus on the sensations of your breath and let go of any distractions.

- ✓ *Action Plan:* Set aside 5-10 minutes each day to practice mindfulness meditation. Find a quiet space where you can sit comfortably and focus on your breath.

Random Acts of Kindness: Perform a random act of kindness for someone else. This could be as simple as complimenting a stranger or helping a friend in need. Acts of kindness can boost your mood and create a ripple effect of positivity.

Action Plan: Look for opportunities to perform random acts of kindness throughout your day. Keep track of your acts of kindness and reflect on how they make you feel.

Goal Setting: Set realistic goals related to developing a cheerful mindset. This could include goals such as practicing gratitude daily, engaging in mindfulness exercises regularly, or seeking support from a therapist or counselor.

- ✓ *Action Plan:* Write down your goals and break them down into smaller, manageable steps. Set deadlines for each step and track your progress. Celebrate your successes along the way.

By incorporating these exercises and action plans into your daily life, you can develop a more cheerful mindset and experience the many benefits of positivity. Remember, developing a positive outlook is a journey, and it's okay to have setbacks along the way. The key is to stay committed to your goals and practice self-compassion as you work towards developing a more positive mindset.

A MASTER-at-a-GLANCE ACTION PLAN
to Develop a Cheerful Mind

Step 1: Define Your Vision

Define what a cheerful mind means to you. What does it look like? How does it feel?

- ✓ Example: A cheerful mind for me means being able to find joy in everyday moments and maintain a positive outlook, even in challenging times.

Step 2: Set Clear Goals

Set specific, achievable goals for developing a cheerful mind. These could be daily, weekly, or monthly goals.

- ✓ Example: My goal for this week is to practice gratitude every day and notice how it impacts my mood.

Step 3: Identify Potential Challenges

Anticipate challenges that may arise in developing a cheerful mind, such as negative thought patterns or external stressors.

- ✓ Example: I know that I tend to be hard on myself, so I may struggle with self-compassion.

Step 4: Develop Strategies

Develop strategies to overcome these challenges, such as practicing self-compassion, reframing negative thoughts, and seeking support from others.

- ✓ Example: When I notice negative self-talk, I will pause and replace it with a positive affirmation.

Step 5: Take Action

Implement your strategies consistently. Take small, manageable steps toward developing a cheerful mind.

- ✓ Example: I will start each day by writing down three things I'm grateful for and reflecting on how they make me feel.

Step 6: Monitor Your Progress

Regularly assess your progress toward developing a cheerful mind. Notice any changes in your mood, outlook, or behavior.

- ✓ Example: After a week of practicing gratitude, I will reflect on how it has impacted my overall mood and well-being.

Step 7: Adjust Your Approach

Be flexible and willing to adjust your approach as needed. If a strategy is not working, try something different.

- ✓ Example: If practicing gratitude doesn't seem to be helping, I will try incorporating more mindfulness into my daily routine.

Step 8: Celebrate Your Successes

Celebrate your progress and achievements, no matter how small. Acknowledge the effort you've put in and the positive changes you've made.

- ✓ Example: I will treat myself to a relaxing evening after completing my first week of practicing gratitude.

By following this MASTER at a GLANCE ACTION PLAN, readers can develop a cheerful mind and cultivate a more positive outlook on life. Remember that developing a cheerful mind is a journey, and it's okay to have setbacks along the way. The key is to stay committed to your goals and strategies, and to practice self-compassion and patience with yourself.

Conclusion:
Developing a Cheerful Mind

As you reach the end of '**The Cheerful Mindset: *Cultivating a Joyful Outlook Everyday***' I hope you have found the strategies and insights shared in these pages to be helpful and inspiring. Cultivating a cheerful mindset is a journey that requires dedication, but the rewards are immense.

Throughout this book, you have learned about the importance of positivity, the benefits of maintaining a cheerful mindset, and practical strategies for fostering a positive outlook. You have discovered how to overcome challenges, maintain positivity in various situations, and celebrate your progress along the way.

Remember, developing a cheerful mind is not about ignoring or denying the challenges and difficulties of life. Instead, it is about facing them with optimism, resilience, and a positive attitude. It is about choosing to focus on the good in life, even when things seem bleak.

As you continue on your journey towards a more cheerful mind, I encourage you to be patient and compassionate with yourself. Change takes time, and setbacks are a natural part of the process. The key is to stay committed to your goals and to continue practicing the strategies outlined in this book.

I hope that '**The Cheerful Mindset: *Cultivating a Joyful Outlook Everyday***' has inspired you to embrace positivity, gratitude, and joy in your life. May you continue to cultivate a cheerful mindset and experience the many benefits it brings, including greater resilience, improved well-being, and deeper connections with others.

Thank you for joining me on this journey. Here's to a future filled with happiness, positivity, and a cheerful mind!

About the Author
'GERARD ASSEY'

Gerard Assey is a Graduate in Economics, a PGD in Management (HRD) and holds a Doctorate in Leadership. Gerard holds several International Qualifications in Sales, Debt Collection, Training & Teaching, and is a 'Fellow' of the prestigious 'Institute of Sales & Marketing Management'-UK, a Certified NLP Practitioner, a 'Certified Trainer', an 'Accredited Management Teacher-Behavioral Sciences', a 'Certified Competency Facilitator', a 'Certified Management Consultant'- (the International credentials of a professional management consultant, awarded in accordance with global standards of the ICMCI); and a Certification from the University of Michigan in 'Successful Negotiation: Essential Strategies and Skills'

He is also a Member of the 'National Association of Sales Professionals' backed with several years experience in varied industries, both in India and Overseas. He also holds an 'Etiquette Consultant' Certification from the USA (by Sue Fox, Author of Best Seller: 'Business Etiquette for Dummies'. She has trained some of the top celebrities' world over). He was also a recipient of a scholarship for extensive training in Japan on 'Corporate Management for India'.

Gerard Assey is 'Founder & Chief Corporate Trainer' of the Group: '**Citius, Altius, Fortius Unlimited'**- an organization that **celebrated 20 years of Glorious Service** in 2021, focusing on 3 Core Competencies:

People. Performance. Profit; in functional areas of Sales & Marketing, HR & Organizational Development, covering Recruitment, Training & Consultancy!

Having managed organizations with large Sales Forces in India & Overseas, his specialization cover extensive areas of Sales Training (All levels - Presentation, Negotiation, Key/ Strategic Accounts Management & Managerial Skills for all sectors), Bid Proposal/ Capture Planning/ Management Trainings, Retail Sales, Customer Service & Customer Retention Programs, Training for Prevention & Collection of Debt, Self & Personal Development Programs (Time Management, Teamwork & Team Building, Business Etiquette & Personal Grooming, Leadership & Managerial Skills, People Management Skills, Train-the-Trainer etc), including preparation of Custom-designed Business Manuals for Internal (HR, Induction, and Sales etc) & External use (Instruction, User Manuals).

Gerard has successfully conducted over 6450 Trainings & Workshops (as of May '25) all across India, Middle East, Africa, Europe & S.E. Asia. Besides public programs conducted regularly, both in India & Overseas, he has some of the top names as clients whom he services from Single Owners to large Public & Government undertakings, covering all sectors, for their in-house needs.

His website: www.CollectionSkills.com is the only one in this part of the world to be featured in the 'Collections & Credit Risk Magazine-USA' under 'Who's Who in Training' and ranks TOP, along with other websites listed below on most search engines.

Gerard is author of 201 Books already (July 2025), all the books being available on all online platforms and outlets as E-books and Paperbacks

A few of our business related books:

1. Bite-sized Bits on Commonsense Management
2. Heart to Heart on Life's Principles'
3. How to become a Successful Manager
4. The Sales Professionals' Master Workbook of S.Y.S.T.E.M.S
5. The Professional Business Email Etiquette Handbook & Guide
6. The Professional Business Video-Conferencing Etiquette Handbook & Guide
7. Professional Presentation Skills
8. Exceptional Customer Service
9. Professional Tele-Marketing Skills
10. Professional Debt Collection Skills
11. The G.R.E.A.T. Sales & Service Workbook
12. Sales Training Advantage for Results (*The Ultimate Sales Training Manual to enable you stand out as a S.T.A.R.*)
13. CEO Daily Planner & Organizer
14. The Sales Professionals' Master Daily Planner
15. The Professional Debt Collector's Master Daily Planner
16. My Daily Planner & Organizer
17. MY EMERGENCY INFORMATION RECORD (Family Emergency & Peace of Mind Planner)
18. The Ultimate Therapist & Counselors Planner and Organizer
19. Building an Ethical Workplace
20. Managing Relationships at Work
21. Managing Business Meetings Effectively
22. Effective Delegation Skills
23. Goal Setting for Success
24. B2B Selling by Email
25. Professional Business Etiquette & Grooming
26. Dining Etiquette & Table Manners
27. Effective Networking Skills
28. Grooming, Etiquette & Manners for Teens, Young Adults & Future Leaders
29. Inter-Personal Skills
30. Get Ready, Get Hired!
31. Selling in a Recession
32. Effective Receivables Management in an Economic Downturn!
33. Real Estate & Property Sales Training
34. Credit Sales & Accounts Receivable Management

35. Selling Skills for Real Estate & Property Advisors
36. Take G.R.E.A.T. C.A.R.E!
37. Spa, Salon & Health Club Selling Skills
38. Selling Travel, Holiday & MICE Services
39. Selling Skills for Spa's, Salons & Health Clubs
40. Retailing in Salons & Spas
41. Selling Holiday, Vacation, Tours & Packages
42. The Power of Sales Referrals
43. Selling Luxury
44. Technical Selling Skills
45. Financial Advisors Sales Training
46. Dealing with Burnout at Work Monopolize Your Markets
47. Selling to Affluent Customers
48. Growing up with Grace
49. Financial Selling Skills
50. *The Effective Manager's Guide: Key Skills to Thrive*
51. From Aspiring to Inspiring: A Guide for New Managers on the Rise
52. The Power of Focus
53. Selling with Integrity: Sell Like Jesus The Perfect Role Model!
54. 31 Habits of Champions: Your 31-Day Journey to Greatness
55. Rejecting Grasshopper Talk: From Grasshopper to Giant-Killer-*Defeating Giants Daily!*
56. Navigate the AI-Powered Future of Bid & Proposals: Up-Skill to Stay Relevant with Alternative Career Paths & Opportunities
57. Hiring Sales Winners
58. Present with Impact
59. Success Unlocked: *Breaking Free from Habits that Hold You Back*
60. Complaints to Cheers, Feedback to Gold: Mastering Complaints Management
61. Thriving Together: *Cultivating Diversity, Equity, and Inclusion*
62. Coaching Skills for Sales Managers
63. Soaring to Success in Business & Leadership: Swifter, Higher, Stronger!
64. From Classroom to Podium: A Student's Guide to Powerful Public Speaking & Presentation Skills
65. Developing Self-Discipline
66. The CEO's 31-Day Power Plan: Unlocking Success through Essential Traits

67. Credibility Matters
68. A Winning Attitude
69. Bid & Proposal Management Using AI
70. Sales Forecasting: A Practical & Proven Guide to Strategic Sales Forecasting
71. Elevate & Energize: *50 Dynamic & Fun Activities for Peak Workplace Morale*
72. 'Sales SOS! Sales on Fire! *30 Days to Conquer Chaos & the Nightmares of Success!'*
73. Mastering Sales Managerial Skills: *Building High-Performing Teams & Driving Exceptional Results*
74. Eagle-Eyed Leadership: Unleashing the Power of 31 Lessons from Eagles
75. The Ultimate Employee Training Guide: *Training Today, Leading Tomorrow*
76. Being More Accountable at Work
77. Creating a Culture of Continuous Improvement
78. Effective Questioning & Listening Skills
79. The Power of Value Selling
80. The Growth Mindset
81. Mastering Professional Help Desk Skills
82. The Power to Lead with Empathy
83. Being Prepared: The Key to Unlocking Success
84. Youthful Spark-Youth Energizers, Activities and Games-Igniting the Fun in Youth
85. Ignite your Motivation for Success
86. Elevate Your Executive Presence: *Your Roadmap to Executive Excellence*
87. Smart Decisions: *Mastering Problem Solving with Strategic Solutions for Business Success*
88. Strategic Planning: *Developing and Implementing Strategic Plans to Achieve Long-Term Business Goals*
89. The Power of Stay Interviews
90. Developing G.R.I.T.
91. Adaptability
92. Diagnosis- *A Key Skill for Leadership*
93. The Burnout-Proof Salesperson: *The Master Guide to Preventing Stress & Burnout-* Strategies for Thriving in Sales
94. Learning from Failure: *Keys to Success*
95. Customer Success Management
96. Overcoming the Killers of Motivation
97. The C-Suite Code: *Mastering Skills for Executive Excellence'*

98. Dealing with Difficult Customers
99. Unlocking Your Potential: Mastering the Top 20 Life Skills for a Brighter Future
100. Nurturing Tomorrow's Leaders: *Essential Soft Skills Every Child Must Learn*
101. Lively & Fun Party Games for Seniors & Elders
102. Role Playing for Sales Champions: From Practice to Performance
103. Fun and Exciting Party Games for Kids
104. Case Studies for Sales
105. Role-Playing for Unbeatable Customer Service
106. Case Studies in Customer Service
107. Case Studies in Winning Negotiations
108. Case Studies in Management & Leadership
109. Case Studies in Human Resources & Talent Management
110. CEO Success Blueprint: The Essential Toolkit for CEOs and C-Level Executives
111. The Salesperson's Self-Coaching Guide: *Master Your Own Self-Coaching Plan for Success*
112. Overcoming Procrastination: *Your Ultimate Guide to Stop Delaying and Start Living Your Best Life*
113. When True Colors Are Exposed: *The Journey to Unmasking Humanity*
114. Life-Changing Habits for Teens: Teen Success Blueprint for a Bright Future
115. Workplace Stress-Free: *Proven Strategies to Thrive at Work and Beyond*
116. Objection Overruled: *The Ultimate Guide to Turning 'No' into 'Yes'*
117. Building Strong Teams: *A Comprehensive Guide to Team Building*
118. Ethical & Moral Leadership in Business: *Eliminating Unethical Practices & Building a Culture of Trust & Integrity*
119. Rising Strong: Building Positive: High Self-Esteem for a Fulfilling Life-*A Practical Guide for Students, Employees, Leaders & Entrepreneurs*
120. The Cheerful Mindset: Cultivating a Joyful Outlook Everyday

From the Ministry side, Gerard graduated in the very first batch of Charis Bible College-India & had for over 9 years served as a Part-time Faculty at Charis Bible College-Chennai (Andrew Wommack Ministries-Colorado, USA).
He also holds a Diploma in Worship (a subject closest to his heart) from the JSOW and is also a graduate of the Advanced Mentorship Program (AMP) and the Circle Of Ministerial Engagement (C.O.M.E.) of Prophet Jerome Fernando and a Spiritual Son of the Esteemed Prophet.
An accomplished author of several Secular & Christian Books, Gerard has been on the board of a few international organizations and boasts of being the SON of the MOST HIGH GOD: An ordinary guy following an extraordinary GOD!

...And some of his most recent Christian Books being:

1. A Bouquet of Praises for My KING
2. Christian Jokes for the Serious Religious' Folks!
3. Jesus Healed You!
4. Praise24Ever! (also in Tamil version)
5. The 5G Network of GOD
6. Building Faith over F.E.A.R- FACE EVERYTHING AND RISE with JESUS
7. Hebrew and Greek Praise and Worship Words
8. Godly Mothers' and Grandmothers' Bible Story time for Kids!
9. Miracles of Jesus in Pictures
10. Raise your Praise all 365 Days
11. Thanking GOD with an Attitude of Gratitude
12. Meditating on the Attributes of GOD
13. Puppet Scripts
14. Alcohol Ruins, JESUS Reforms, Renews & Restores!
15. Habakkuk 2:2 Christian Daily Journal, Planner & Organizer
16. ABC of GOD's Word for Handwriting Practice
17. Daily Bible Verse Handwriting Practice (Building Godly Character & Faith through Cursive Handwriting Practice!)
18. Guiding Light: Fun & Faith-Building Bible Activities for Children
19. Rejecting Grasshopper Talk: From Grasshopper to Giant-Killer-*Defeating Giants Daily!*
20. Teen Titans of Faith: *Building Courage, Determination & Christ-like-Esteem*
21. I AM Empowered: *Unleashing Divine Power with Positive Declarations*

22. Be A Solution Provider-*From Passion to Purpose*: *A Biblical Guide to Being the Answer to the World!*
23. Miracles of JESUS
24. Parables of Jesus for a Meaningful Life!
25. A Grateful Heart: Importance of Sharing Testimonies of GOD's Grace
26. Melodies of Worship to JESUS: 31 Songs of Praise & Worship From My Heart to HIS!
27. I AM SO BLESSED!
28. My Daily Cup of Energizer
29. 31 Leadership Lessons *from* Jesus- *The Supreme Leader*
30. Peace Amidst Storms: A Biblical Guide to Conquering S.T.R.E.S.S.
31. Rise Above: 20 Biblical Eagle Lessons for Life's Triumphs
32. Godly Goal Setting: *The FAITHFUL Blueprint for a Purpose-Driven Life*
33. The Profound Attributes of our Mighty GOD: Understanding the 10S's of the Almighty
34. Worship Now, Worship Forever: *A Journey from Earthly Praise to Eternal Glory*
35. Unceasing Praise & Worship: *365 Days to Worship the King*
36. The ROAR Within: *Living with Purpose and Authority through the Power of the Holy Spirit*
37. From Potential to Purpose: Unlocking and Multiplying Your Talents & Gifts for Kingdom Impact
38. Songs from the Heart: *Worshipping GOD in Your Own Tune & Melody*
39. Awakening Praise & Worship: Hebrew & Greek Words to Raise Your Praise
40. Sing a NEW Song to the LORD Everyday: *Daily Devotions of Praise & Worship to Lift Your Heart & Glorify HIS Name*
41. *The* A.R.O.M.A. of True Worship: *Creating Worship That Delights God*
42. Becoming A Kingdom Champion: *Embracing God's Call for a Life of Purpose & Victory*
43. The Busy Businessman's Daily Devotional: 366 Crisp Truths to Start Your Day Strong
44. The Teacher's Heart: *Daily Devotions for Educators*
45. Anchored! *A 31-Day Devotional for Students Facing Life's Challenges*
46. Suddenly! Unlocking Unorthodox Breakthroughs through Unusual Worship
47. Overcoming Adversity: *Lessons from the Bible for Modern*

Challenges

48. LORD, Don't do it without me
49. Kingdom Leadership: *Biblical Principles for Modern Leaders*
50. Heartprints of God- *Growing God's Way:* Daily Devotions for Kids to Shine Bright
51. Send Judah First: Let your Praises Go up First to See the Mighty Move of GOD
52. DIVINE MOMENTS: *Recognizing, Embracing, Preparing, and Walking into Life-Changing Encounters with God*
53. Be a Builder in the Kingdom: *The C.E.M.E.N.T. Guide to Creating a Lasting Legacy*
54. Unshakable: *Pillars of Godly Womanhood* (Pillars of Faith That Changed History)
55. Lead Like a Shepherd: *14 Essential Traits for Pastoral Excellence*
56. The Worship Leader's Arsenal: *Powerful Exhortations to Ignite Thanksgiving, Praise & Worship*
57. Women of UnShakable Faith: *31-Day Devotional for Strength, Purpose & Influence*
58. Called to Teach: *A Complete 10-Week Training Guide for Impactful VBS Teachers*
59. Strumming for the KING: Cowboy Songs of Faith & Fire
60. The Ultimate Youth Camp Playbook: *50 Bible-Centered Indoor Games to Engage, Equip, and Empower Teens*
61. Glad in HIS Presence: *David's Revelation of GOD's Love & Mercy*
62. The Spirit Behind the Sound: *52 Devotionals for Worship Teams*
63. THE COWBOY'S COMPASS: *Riding the Trail of Faith with Grit & Grace*
64. Worship as My Weapon: *Living Victoriously through the Power of Praise*
65. A Worshipper Always Wins: *Living a Life of Victorious Worship*
66. Worship That Leads to the Throne: *Practical Strategies for Worship Leaders to Inspire Their Team & Usher People into God's Presence*
67. Worship as Warfare: *Conquering through the Sound of Surrender*
68. Watchmen on the Walls: *A 31-Day Devotional for Worship Teams*
69. KINGDOM BUSINESS: *52 Biblical Principles for GODLY*

Leadership & Wise Decisions

70. From Evening to Morning: *Rediscovering GOD's Sacred Hours*
71. Waves of Glory: *Worship through Dance, Flags, Staff & Sound*
72. WORSHIP TEAM BUILDER: *Guiding Your Team from Formation to Fruitfulness*
73. The Worship Leader's Master Training Manual

Besides regularly contributing to business & trade journals, including international ones such as the 'Creative Training Techniques' and the 'Sales News' of the U.S.A, He is also a member of several prestigious bodies & trade associations, having participated in many Conferences & Workshops in India & Overseas.

Prior to his last assignment of leading & managing a large MNC as head, Gerard had a 3-year stint in the Middle East as a Consultant with a leading British Consultancy Firm.

As the past 'Official Country Representative' for the International Business Award- 'THE STEVIES'-(the business world's own Oscar) for about 4 years- he ensured a few Indian companies that qualify for the same every year!

Gerard can be contacted at:
Email: training@Sales-Training.in,training@CollectionSkills.com
Websites:

www.Sales-Training.in
www.EtiquetteWorks.in
www.CollectionSkills.com
www.RetailSalesTraining.in
www.SalesTrainingIndia.com
www.ManualPreparation.com
www.TrainingWithPuppets.com
www.FirstContactAcademy.com
www.SalesAndMarketingRecruiter.com